The Sorcerer's Apprentice
METHUEN CHILDREN'S BOOKS
INK

Books told and illustrated by Tomi Ungerer

I AM PAPA SNAP AND THESE ARE MY FAVOURITE NO SUCH STORIES

Available in hardback and paperback:

THE THREE ROBBERS · NO KISS FOR MOTHER · CRICTOR · MOON MAN

Printed in Great Britain
ISBN 0 416 080804 (HB)   0 416 46830 6 (PB)

Long, long ago there lived a sorcerer – a wise old wizard – who could weave the most marvellous magic spells. He could turn princes into field mice, pebbles into pure gold, and he could make himself disappear – *Presto!* – in a puff of pale blue powder.

The sorcerer lived in a castle high above the River Rhine. The castle had tall towers, twisted turrets and a maze of vaulted passageways which led to a deep, dank cellar.

VI
XII
VI
W.C

The cellar was the sorcerer's workshop. One side of the cellar was lined with shelves of musty, dusty, leather-bound books. By far the most important book of all was an enormous volume called *Complete Magic Spells and Incantations*. It contained the sorcerer's secrets: all his charms and conjurations, all his rites and rituals, and all his symbols and secret words.

This book stood alone on the top shelf, where it was guarded day and night by an old blue-eyed owl. The book was always locked, and the sorcerer always wore the key around his neck.

On the other side of the cellar was the sorcerer's laboratory. There stood the sorcerer's kiln, his cosmic oven, and the distillery where he made secret chemical concoctions. And there, too, were all the other tools of the sorcerer's trade: cauldrons and kettles, flagons and flasks, alantirs and ampulars, bubbling beakers and vapour-filled vessels – and piles of phosphorescent stones ready to be pulverized into magic powders and potions.

In the middle of the workshop was a water tub. Every day the tub had to be filled. Heavy buckets of water had to be brought all the way up the steep stone steps which led from the River Rhine.

Carrying all those buckets was the job of the sorcerer's apprentice – a likeable, but sometimes lazy, lad named Humboldt.

Humboldt wanted to be a sorcerer too, some day, and so he worked at the castle in return for lessons in magic. He loved the lessons, but he hated the chores, especially carrying bucket after bucket of water.

The sorcerer paid no attention to Humboldt's grumbles.

"An apprentice must *earn* his magic powers," he said.

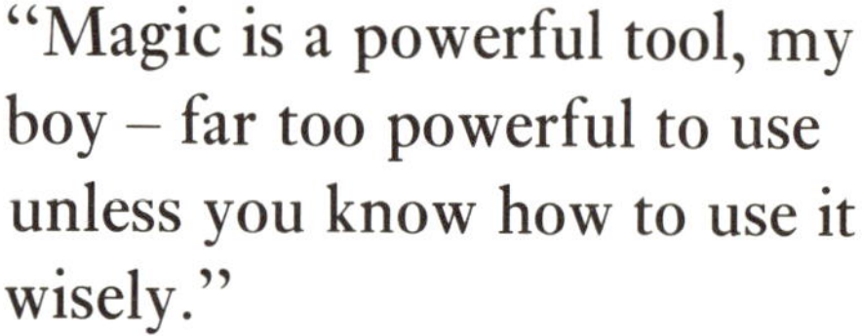

"Magic is a powerful tool, my boy – far too powerful to use unless you know how to use it wisely."

One day the sorcerer was invited to a wizards' conclave. Before going, he copied some words out of the big book of magic.

"When I return," he said, "I expect to find the water tub filled all the way up – to the *brim*, Humboldt!"

I II III IV V
CRICTOR

Then the sorcerer covered himself with his cloak and mumbled a few magic words, and disappeared – *Pfffffft!* – in a puff of pale blue powder – which promptly settled all over the furniture and the floor.

"It isn't fair," grumbled Humboldt. "Why should I slave all day when the master could cast one magic spell and have all the chores done in an instant. Magic's a much easier way, and much more fun, too!"

Hopelessly, Humboldt looked around at the dirt and dust, and as he looked, a shiny object caught his eye.

There on the sorcerer's work table was the gold key to the big book of magic. The sorcerer had been in such a hurry he had forgotten it. What luck!

Humboldt grabbed the key. Then he looked at the top library shelf to make sure the old owl was asleep. It was.

Quickly, Humboldt steadied the library ladder and climbed to the top. His hands shook with excitement as he unlocked the big red and gold book. Making as little noise as possible, Humboldt flipped through the parchment pages. There were circles and stars and mysterious symbols. Most of the words were in a language Humboldt couldn't understand.

Then he saw, under the heading PRACTICAL MAGIC, "*Broom, magic – How to make a stick fulfil all the wishes of your will.*"

"That means the broom will do anything I ask," thought Humboldt happily. So he said the words over and over till he knew them by heart.

Then he closed the book, fastened his eyes on the old straw broom in the corner of the cellar, and called out: SHARRRROOM TA!
VARRRROOM BA!
Old broom perk,
Bring water
And do all my work.

The old owl awakened with a flurry and a flapping of wings, and batted the boy off the ladder.

The ladder crashed and broke in two. But luckily Humboldt landed unhurt, cushioned by the sorcerer's stuffed crocodile.

He lay there stunned.

Nothing happened. Had he said the wrong magic words?

No! Look! The broom moved.

Then it flipped on its end. Hop. Hop.

Hooray! The magic words were right.

Humboldt pointed to a water bucket.

Hop. Hop. The broom hopped over, bent and picked up the bucket. Then it hopped across the cellar floor, out of the castle door and down the steep stone steps to the River Rhine.

At the water's edge, the broom tipped, dipped the bucket into the water, and filled it. Then it turned and hopped all the way back up the steep stone steps.

The broom poured the water into the tub. Then it hobbled and bobbled back to the river.

"Hooray!" Humboldt shouted with delight. He daydreamed happily of being a great sorcerer, while the water went on hobbling and bobbling.

All at once Humboldt noticed that the water was up to the top of the tub.

"Stop, broom!" he called. "That's enough."

But the broom didn't stop. It kept right on emptying buckets into the tub. Water trickled over the rim and sloshed on the floor. It drenched the rug and made a big sloppy puddle by the cellar door. The sorcerer's cat, who hated to get her paws wet, yowled in rage.

Humboldt was frightened. "*Stop, broom!*" he cried out again. "Broom, you've *got* to stop. Do as I say, *broom. Obey!*"

But the broom *didn't* stop. It kept right on hobbling and bobbling and bringing more water.

The water rose higher and higher. The puddle by the door became a pond. The fire in the oven went out with a hiss.

Humboldt couldn't stop what he had started. And he couldn't look in the magic book again because the ladder was broken. He was frantic.

"Woe! Oh, misery!" he whined. "What will my master do when he sees what I've done? Oh, why did I look in the magic book! If only I can remember some of the magic words, maybe the broom will stop."

Hoping they were like the words that had *started* the broom working, Humboldt called out:

SHARRRROOM TA! VARRRROOM BA!
Old broom stop your hopping. Do as I say.

Nothing happened. So he tried again:

SHARRRROOM TA! VARRRROOM BA!
Go back broom. Stop hopping. You must obey.

But the broom didn't stop. It kept right on hobbling and bobbling and bringing buckets of water. No *other* combination of words worked, either. Not even saying the *Varrrroom ba!* before the *Sharrrroom ta!* Not anything.

The water was now waist high. The cat was climbing the furniture and the snakes were slithering up the draperies. Scared and soaked to the skin, Humboldt knew he had to do *some*thing to stop the broom. He grabbed the sorcerer's axe.

Crack! Whack! He cut the broom in two.

"Aha! broom! I've got you at last," Humboldt cried out. "Got you for good. Your magic won't get me into any more trouble."

But even as he said it, something amazing and unbelievable and horrible happened.

The two pieces of the broom quivered. Then they both tipped, flipped over, and started hopping. Then each of them picked up a bucket and went bumping and thumping down the steep stone steps to the River Rhine.

Even more awful, all the broom *splinters* did the same thing. Soon there was a procession of hundreds of brooms, big and little and in-between, all hobbling and bobbling, all thumping and bumping, all bringing buckets of water from the river.

By now the flood had reached the top shelf of the bookcase. Humboldt was swimming for his life.

The cat and the owl were clinging to the chandelier and screeching in fury. Cauldrons were slamming and kettles were banging. All the magic powders and potions were washed into the flood waters, turning them pink and purple and gentian violet.

And still all the brooms kept hobbling and bobbling and bringing water.

Soon water was everywhere: whirling, swirling, curling into whirlpools; rushing, gushing, pushing the animals; drowning, surrounding, pounding the furniture.

"Help!" Humboldt cried. "Help, master, I'm going to drown!"

Suddenly there was a blinding flash of light. *Presto!* The sorcerer appeared at the top of the steps. He bellowed angrily,

"HALT TA! SCHTALT BA!
Old broom to the corner. Cessare!"

Slowly, the water subsided.

Slowly, Humboldt floated to the floor.

"Mmmmmmmaster, it was only a joke," Humboldt muttered feebly. "Pl–pl–please don't punish me."

"Ha!" said the sorcerer, his eyes flashing fire. Then he pointed to the water bucket.

Waterlogged and bone weary, the sorcerer's apprentice walked to the corner. He bent to pick up the empty bucket.

And as Humboldt bent, the broom in the corner tipped and flipped over. *Slap! Whack! Bang! Crack!* It gave Humboldt four sharp whacks on the backside – which sent the sorcerer's apprentice flying all the way down the steep stone steps to the River Rhine.

AND THAT WAS THAT!